BEING A REFLECTIVE TEACHER

DR. RENI FRANCIS

"We do not learn from experience ... we learn from reflecting on experience."

John Dewey

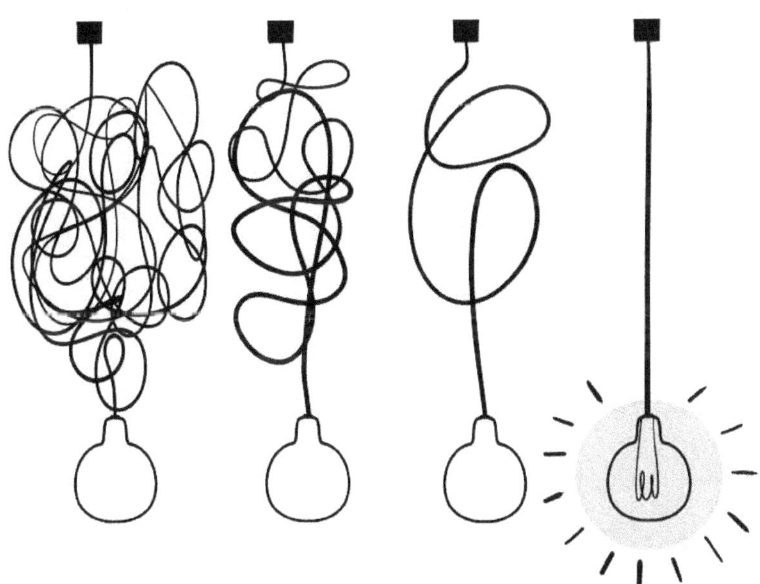

Contents

Acknowledgements

As water reflects a face, so a man's heart reflects the man.

Proverbs 27:19

Being a Reflective Teacher is a very crucial topic to every teacher. Every classrrom is a stage of various activities, teaching-learning process, enhancing intrapersonal and interpersonal skills, social engagement and many more. These varied expressions give numerous experiences, these experiences maybe sometimes good or sometimes need due attention for corrective steps. Reflective practices comes as an aid in this process of transforming your actions to a fruitful experiences.

Being a Reflective teacher is not only the tool in the hands for a teacher but also the exposure that the teacher provides to the students. Reflection is process of introspection. Introspection leads to deep thinking, critical thinking, creative thinking, problem solving, decision making thus helping an individual to a wide spectrum of ideas for possible new actions or steps. Providing an opportunity for Reflection is the need of the hour. There is no age limit for Reflection and not constrained to any group of people. It is open for all and at all times. Reflection leads to refinemnet of thoughts to a desirable action. Lets start this process of reflection in our lives today and see the difference we make in our life and the life of of people around us.

My views on reflective practices and classroom experiences are from my personal experiences and I thank each one of you to help me enhance reflective practices in my life and share my experiences.

Thank you all.

Enjoy reading

1

Reflection in Teaching

Effective instruction is essential to the success of students—not just occasionally, but every day in every classroom and school. The academic, physical, social, emotional, and behavioural well-being of students is influenced by effective teaching. When all the education stakeholders, including parents, policymakers, members of the community, and educators, share responsibility for student achievement and continuous improvement, teaching is most effective. Effective professional development is the single most crucial means of promoting effective practices by teachers in the classroom. A clear vision for teaching and learning is what leads to consistently excellent instruction in every classroom, every school, and every day. The vision is then incorporated into an instructional framework that specifies precise performance outcomes for students and teachers. Every professional learning system is built on these framework and outcomes in achieving quality standards in education.

The ways in which students learn and the role that teaching plays in achieving the learning outcomes are described as a vital goal for teaching and learning. These are built on strong foundation of learning theories and models chosen to explain how students learn, who they are, and the environment in which they learn. Stakeholders from across the learning community come together to plan the kind of education that will best prepare students for the future. Effective teaching necessitates more than just the creation of a vision, an instructional framework, and student learning objectives. In addition to explicit performance standards for educators, processes for enhancing and evaluating effective practice are necessary for effective teaching. Teachers' performance standards specify the standards for their instruction, individual development, and effective evaluation.

An instructional framework, standards for student learning, performance expectations for educators, and a convergence of state, school system, and classroom policy, planning, and goals are all necessary for effective teaching. These components, which form the foundation of effective teaching, are developed and implemented in collaboration by educators, policymakers, community members, and decision makers. By creating a culture of collaboration and shared accountability, it is possible to ensure that every educator participates in meaningful professional development. Teaching success is a process rather than a destination. Teachers face new challenges to improve and expand their teaching methods each year. Teachers encounter new students with diverse learning requirements each year. In order to speed up learning, they strive to incorporate cutting-edge technology into their classrooms. Student learning benchmarks continue to evolve. Effective instruction is the subject of new research. The only way to ensure that these difficulties become opportunities to enhance student and educator performance is through professional learning systems. Effective designs encourage active participation and teamwork through the integration of learning theories and research. The expected outcomes, preferences of students, experience levels, school culture, and other factors all influence learning designs. Mentoring, coaching, and team learning that focuses on clearly defined outcomes for teachers *and their students improve teaching practices. Hence it gives emergence to pedagogy.*

The study of teaching and learning in accordance with established educational objectives is referred to as pedagogy. There are two parties involved in the teaching-learning process: the student and the teacher. The two are able to communicate through pedagogy. It involves the methods that the teacher will use to teach a lesson and the methods that will be used to measure how well the information is received by the student.

Educationists view pedagogy as a tool for effective teaching and learning and have developed a variety of effective pedagogical practices to improve student-teacher interaction.

The strategies and methods teachers use to ensure the achievement of the goal are referred to as "pedagogical" when they are used in teaching-learning sessions. Educational psychology and child psychology have a big impact on pedagogy. It examines the responses of students in addition to improving educational delivery methods. Overall, its primary goal is to create effective learning environments.

Over the course of many decades, education has undergone a significant transformation. More students can access it than ever before. Additionally, formal education is now accessible via technology-enabled channels in a wide range of learning fields and for a wide range of student population. This has been possible due to the pedagogical practices' ability to adapt to the ever-changing world. Therefore, when it comes to providing high-quality education, efficient pedagogical strategies are of the utmost importance.

Students are able to achieve learning outcomes and realize their full educational potential when pedagogical strategies are used effectively. Strong learning foundations are provided by high-quality teaching pedagogy. It helps students learn advanced skills and concepts. Additionally, teachers can monitor their students' academic progress with the right pedagogy. The significance of pedagogy is emphasized in the following points.

- *The quality of instruction can be improved with a well-thought-out pedagogy.*

- *The student is more open to learning as a result, the degree to which the student participates in the teaching-learning process rises as a result of this.*

- *Students with varying learning styles and abilities benefit from education that is delivered through an appropriate pedagogy.*

- *Students gain a deeper comprehension of the material, this ensures that a course learning objectives are met.*

- *Students from disadvantaged groups and those with special needs require an appropriate pedagogical approach, namely minorities or women. Additionally, it encourages them to join the mainstream educational community.*

Students acquire higher-level cognitive skills by way of an example of thoughtfully developed teaching pedagogy, namely applying, analysing, evaluating and creating as per the Revised Bloom's Taxonomy.

An essential component of the learning experience is the correct evaluation of student performance. The most important thing is to grade papers efficiently while being fair to all students.

Tina did a movie review and asked students to identify any one character of the movie and share it with the class. However, the activity did not stimulate interest among the students.

Reflection:

- *Tina's movie review did not stimulate interest because the choice of movie was given to students.*
- *Tina did not specify the genre of movies.*
- *The movie review presented was not in a proper format.*
- *The review expressed did not reveal the need for doing a movie review activity.*

The pedagogy used in the teaching-learning process is influenced by a variety of factors and teaching methods. Subject, curriculum, learning motivation, and instructor competence are few of the vital factors. The pedagogy is also influenced by student learning styles and infrastructure availability.

1.Teacher competence:

Students remain motivated, interested, and eager to learn when they are taught well. Additionally, such a teacher employs a well-balanced combination of knowledge, abilities, and skills.

2. Learner's Learning Styles:

Instructors are able to select the most effective pedagogical strategy by having an understanding of the learning styles of their students. Additionally, a pedagogical strategy that takes into account the various learning styles of the students expedites the learning process. It keeps students interested in learning and motivated.

3.Subject of Study:

The choice of pedagogy is also influenced by the field of study. For instance, physics calls for a combination of classroom instruction and hands-on lab time. In contrast, there is no need for laboratory sessions in political science. In addition to theory and laboratory sessions, architecture calls for field trips.

4.Availbilty of resources:

Equipment like smart classrooms and virtual labs aid in broadening the scope of the learning-teaching cycle. These educational resources keep students engaged and the learning sessions alive.

5.System of Education:

Curriculum standards, policies, and other aspects of an educational system also have an impact on the educational approach. A learning pedagogy that fosters higher-order thinking, for instance, is discouraged by an exam that tests a student's ability to memorize and recall facts.

Effective pedagogical approaches are crucial in the effective delivery of knowledge to learners. The choice of a particular pedagogy depends on many factors, some of which have been discussed above. Also, pedagogy relates teachers, students, and learning with each other. It helps achieve academic outcomes. So, teachers are often advised by educationists to develop their own, unique pedagogical approach. Some pedagogical approaches described below are more general and ubiquitously adopted.

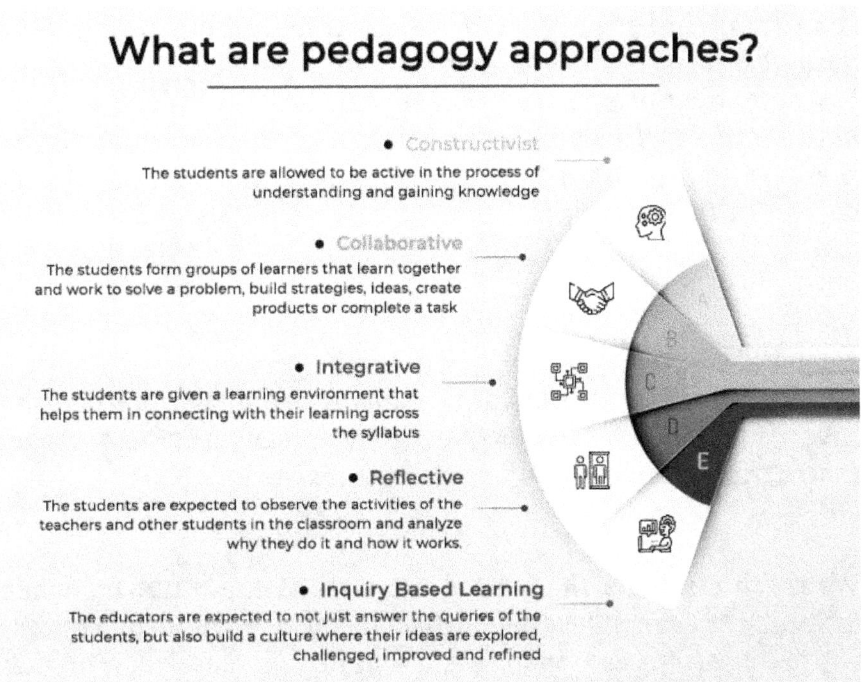

Pedagogy approaches

Based on the factors of learning we need to focus on the basic principles of teaching.

Principles of Teaching:

Teaching is a complex, multifaceted activity that frequently requires instructors to juggle multiple tasks and objectives at once and with flexibility. By assisting us in creating the conditions that support student learning and minimizing the need to revise materials, content, and policies, the succinct but potent set of principles below can help us make teaching both more effective and more efficient. Even though applying these principles takes time and effort, it often saves time and energy in the long run.

1.Learning relevant information about students and applying that information to our course design and classroom instruction is necessary for effective teaching.

We teach students the content as well as the material when we teach. Learning can be affected by a variety of student characteristics. For instance, students' perspectives on the world are influenced by their cultural and generational backgrounds; Students with different disciplinary backgrounds approach problems in different ways; and new learning is shaped by students' prior knowledge, both accurate and inaccurate. Although we are unable to accurately measure all of these characteristics, gathering the most pertinent data as early as possible during course planning and continuing to do so throughout the semester can (a) guide instructional adaptations (e.g., recognition of the need for additional practice), (b) help explain student difficulties (e.g., identification of common misconceptions), and (c) inform course design (e.g., decisions about objectives, pacing, examples, and format).

2.Aligning the three major components of instruction is necessary for effective teaching: assessments, learning objectives, and instructional activities

In the end, doing this in advance saves time and results in a better course of action. When (a) we, as instructors, articulate a clear set of learning objectives (i.e., the knowledge and skills that we expect students to demonstrate by the end of a course), teaching is more effective and student learning is enhanced; (b) The instructional activities, such as case studies, labs, discussions, and readings, provide goal-oriented practice to support these learning objectives; and (c) the assessments—such as tests, papers, problem sets, and performances—offer students opportunities to demonstrate and practice the knowledge and skills outlined in the objectives. Additionally, the assessments allow teachers to provide students with specific feedback that can direct further learning.

3.Clearly articulating expectations regarding learning objectives and policies is necessary for effective teaching.

What is expected of students in different classrooms and even within a particular discipline varies greatly. For instance, the definition of evidence can vary greatly from course to course; In one course, what is acceptable collaboration may be considered cheating in another. As a result, our expectations may not match those of the students. As a result, students learn more and perform better when we explicitly communicate our expectations. Students have a clear goal to aim for and can track their progress as they go by articulating the learning objectives, which are the knowledge and skills they are expected to possess by the end of a course. In a similar vein, making it clear in class and on the syllabus what the policies of the course are—for example, when it comes to class participation, laptop use, and late assignments—helps us come to an early agreement and tends to lessen any potential challenges. All students benefit from a more productive learning environment when teachers are explicit.

4.Teaching well necessitates prioritizing the knowledge and abilities we choose to emphasize.

The enemy is coverage: Avoid trying to complete too much in a single class. We must make decisions—sometimes difficult ones—about what we will and will not include in a course because too many topics hinder student learning. This entails (a) recognizing the course's parameters (such as class size, students' backgrounds and experiences, course position in the curriculum sequence, and number of units), (b) setting our priorities for student learning, and (c) selecting a set of reasonable objectives.

5.Understanding and overcoming our expert blind spots are necessary for effective instruction.

We are not their pupils! When we teach, we frequently skip or combine crucial steps because experts typically access and apply knowledge automatically and unconsciously (e.g., make connections, draw on relevant bodies of knowledge, and choose appropriate strategies).Students, on the other hand, lack the background and experience necessary to make these leaps, so they may become confused, make incorrect judgments, or fail to develop essential skills. They require instructors who can clearly explain connections, break down tasks into component steps, and demonstrate processes in detail. Even though this is difficult for experts to do, we need to identify and explicitly communicate to students the knowledge and abilities we take for granted so that students can observe expert thinking in action and practice putting it into practice for themselves.

6.Adopting appropriate teaching roles to support our learning objectives is necessary for effective teaching.

Even though students are ultimately in charge of their own education, our roles as teachers play a crucial role in influencing students' thinking and behaviour. In our teaching, we can play a variety of roles, such as synthesizer, moderator, challenger, and commentator. The learning objectives and the instructional activities should guide the selection of these roles. For instance, the most effective instructor role might be to frame, direct, and moderate a discussion if the goal is for students to be able to analyze arguments from a written text or case. Our job might be to push students to explain their choices and think about other points of view if the goal is to help them learn how to defend their positions or creative choices when they present their work. Depending on the learning objectives, these roles may remain constant or shift throughout the semester.

7.Teaching well necessitates gradually improving our courses based on feedback and reflection.

Teaching necessitates adaptation. We need to keep thinking about how we teach and be ready to make adjustments if necessary (for example, if something isn't working, we want to try something new, the student population has changed, or new issues in our fields are emerging).We need to look at relevant data on our own teaching effectiveness in order to determine what needs to change and how to implement it. We may need to seek additional feedback with assistance from other teachers/ institutes (e.g., interpreting early course evaluations, conducting focus groups, designing pre- and post-tests) or a lot of this information already exists (e.g., student work, course evaluations from previous semesters, dynamics of class participation).We might change a course's learning objectives, content, structure, or format or our teaching in other ways based on such data. Changes that are purposeful, small, and motivated by our priorities and feedback are most likely to be manageable and effective

15

2

Reflective practices

—♡—

Reflective practice is the ability to reflect on one's actions so as to engage in a process of continuous learning. - Donald Schon

Imagine that you arrive home at the end of a very bad week in which everything has gone wrong. A time machine awaits you at the front door, allowing you to relive the entire week once more by going back to Monday morning. You utilize this chance to contemplate all that turned out badly and what you could do (regardless) to address things as well as attempting to rehash the things that you have done well. Although it may not appear so, this is reflective practice—the act of considering our experiences in order to gain future knowledge from them. You probably won't be able to travel back in time in real life, but you can still work toward becoming a reflective practitioner. We can all engage in activities to reflect on our experiences, gain knowledge from them, and plan our next steps.

As a means of learning from actual life experiences, disciplines like teaching, medicine, and social work developed reflective practice. People who work in these areas would think about their interactions with patients, patients, or clients, how they worked, and what they could have learned from them. When studying, you can use reflection to prepare for group projects or complete assignments. It can also be useful outside of academia when applying for jobs, earning a professional qualification, or just thinking about your job.

Even though a definition of reflective practice was provided above, this is just one step in a much larger process. Different people will define reflection in different ways because it is a very personal thing. It is essential to keep in mind that there is no one "correct" way to define reflection or how it should be carried out because a great deal will depend on your particular circumstances.

Need to reflect

You can practice reflection during your education, within the workplace or as part of your general personal wellbeing. It has many benefits at both a personal and professional level and can help you to focus on planning for future experiences.

• You will probably be very involved in your work and succeeding academically when you are studying. In this situation, it can be easy to become overly focused on your work, but reflective practice lets you see the bigger picture. If you do regular reflection, like once a term, it can help you think about your studying goals and future plans.

• It may assist with the problem of "self-talk. Every one of us has a little voice inside of us that tells us all the things we could have done differently in certain circumstances. When we learn from our mistakes and move forward, reflecting on them can help us use this voice.

• It identifies areas for growth or improvement. You will find that you are constantly asked for ways to improve your knowledge and skills, whether you are a student or working in the workplace. Undertaking reflections can assist you with contemplating regions that you can chip away at as well as the thing you are getting along nicely.

• Assignments and coursework frequently require students to reflect. You may be required to reflect on something as part of a general essay question or to complete an exercise that requires you to consider a topic in relation to your own experiences.

• Reflection can encourage experimentation and creativity. It can be helpful to consider what you are doing and why you are doing it because it is easy to get stuck in a problem. New thoughts and concepts may be sparked as a result of this.

• It is in our nature to make assumptions about other people and situations. You may be able to refute some of these presumptions and gain a fresh perspective by taking a step back and reflecting.

• Emotional intelligence, or the capacity to comprehend and maintain emotional control, relies heavily on reflection. This is a useful skill for both our own well-being and *collaboration.*

· It assists with keeping a good work/life balance by offering a characterized interaction for thoroughly considering things. I hope you can learn from them and move on instead of dwelling on the incident.

Ways to Reflect

Now that you are aware of the advantages of reflection, how do you actually engage in it? There is no one-size-fits-all approach, and what works for your peers may not work for you.Some people find that speaking their thoughts out loud helps them, while others find that it's more private. You can write down your thoughts on a regular basis if you're really organized, or you can do it whenever you can. It's ideal in the event that you can reflect consistently as this will assist you with getting into the propensity and you will actually want to expand on what you realize.

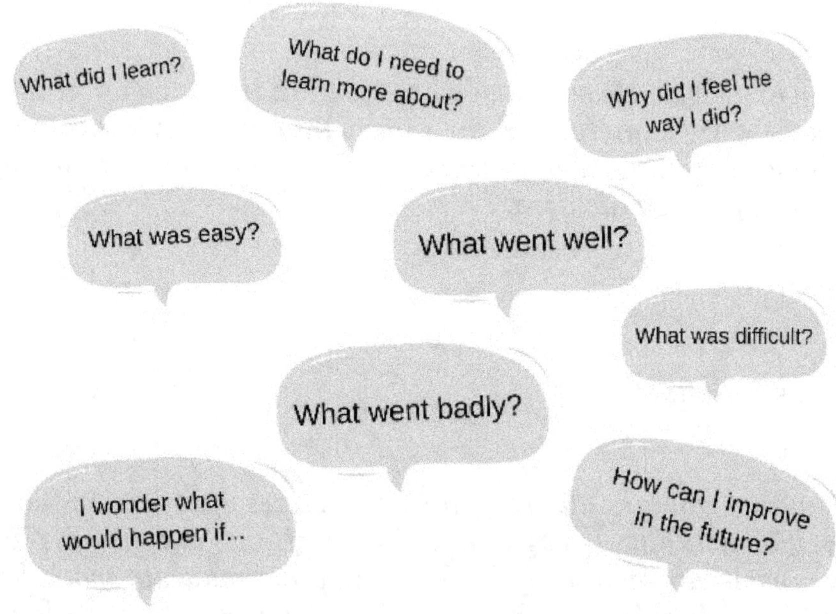

Reflection

Reflective questions

The easiest way to get started with reflection is to ask yourself some of the following questions about the experience you want to reflect on. Think about how you might record your answers, for example in a reflective journal, so that you can remember them in the future.

- *What did I learn?*

- *What do I need to learn more about?*

- *Why did I feel the way I did?*

- *What was easy?*

- *What went well?*

- *What was difficult?*

- *What went badly?*

- *How can I improve in the future?*

- *I wonder what would happen if...*

Sumi was demonstrating Respiratory process in the class through a balloon, but the class was very noisy. Sumi couldn't control the class and the demonstration conducted was ineffective in conveying the topic of Breathing inhale and exhale. Sumi went back home and reflected on the classroom activity.

Reflection:

- *Sumi reflected on the classroom activity and felt that she could give prior instructions in the class before starting the activity.*
- *Maybe also ask for few student volunteers to help in doing the demonstration.*
- *Ask few students to do the experiment.*
- *Few students to note down the process of the experiment.*

Any occasion or moment can inspire reflection. It doesn't have to be written in a formal way, follow a certain format, or even be written in a certain way for it to be valuable.

Whether it is more beneficial to reflect on positive or negative experiences is a common question regarding reflection. There is no right or wrong answer to this question because a lot of what you decide to think about will be determined by your personal circumstances and preferences. However, the majority of people probably do best when they find a balance between the two.

Positive experiences: It can be very uplifting and motivating to reflect on positive experiences. It inspires you to look at what you've been doing well in school and in your career so far and how you can capitalize on this in the future. It is natural to want to repeat our successes, and by looking at what went well, we can come up with a strategy to do so. However, if we only focus on the positive aspects, we may overlook issues, which may result in additional issues in the future.

Negative experiences: Negative experiences are typically easier to learn from because we can dissect them and consider what we can improve. We can always do better, and this is a great starting point for planning for the future. However, it can be demotivating and negative to focus too much on the bad things that happened. As a result, it's critical that you balance the things you look at during your reflections.

Barriers to Reflection

• *You don't have the time: Whether you're working, studying, or both, it can be hard to find time to finish your current list of things to do, so why add another task? Though proper reflection takes time, you should view it as an investment in your education, professional growth, and mental health.*

• *Culture of the organization: Not everyone works for an organization that welcomes reflection, which is particularly challenging in the workplace. It can be difficult to navigate a lack of support from management who do not value reflective practice. Try to explain it in terms of the return on their investment if they provide you with the necessary resources to reflect.*

• *Lack of ability: Many newcomers to reflection are concerned that they are doing it incorrectly or do not know where to begin. Some well-known models of reflection place unrealistic demands on the way the process must be carried out. Keep in mind that reflection is a very individual process and that there is no "right" way to do it.You can follow which at any point course suits you.It may take some trial and error before you discover the method that works best for you, but trying is only half the fun!*

• *Environment: Finding a physical place to reflect can be difficult for some people. To engage in reflective practice, you will need to be in a particular frame of mind, which can make finding a suitable location challenging. While some people prefer a noisy environment, others prefer a quiet one. If you're new to reflection, you might have to try different things to find the right setting, but once you do, you can work on finding a place to practice it.*

• *Motivation: A lack of time and support can hinder your ability to reflect, particularly if you've been working on something all day. Going home at night and contemplating it is the last thing you want to do!*

• *You: might be one of the biggest obstacles to reflection! Sadly, this is one of the most difficult obstacles to overcome, but it is doable. Being reflective necessitates some degree of self-awareness, which can be uncomfortable for some people, particularly those who aren't accustomed to doing so. The good news is that with some practice, this can be done.*

Many people worry that they will be unable to write reflectively but chances are that you do it more than you think! It's a common task during both work and study from appraisal and planning documents to recording observations at the end of a module. The following pages will guide you through some simple techniques for reflective writing as well as how to avoid some of the most common pitfalls.

Reflective writing

Writing reflectively involves critically analysing an experience, recording how it has impacted you and what you plan to do with your new knowledge. It can help you to reflect on a deeper level as the act of getting something down on paper often helps people to think an experience through.

The key to reflective writing is to be analytical rather than descriptive. Always ask why rather than just describing what happened during an experience.

Reflective writing is...

- *Written in the first person*

- *Analytical*

- *Free flowing*

- *Subjective*

- *A tool to challenge assumptions*

- *A time investment*

Reflective writing isn't...

- Written in the third person

- Descriptive

- What you think you should write

- Objective

- A tool to ignore assumptions

- A waste of time

Ravi had to enhance language skills among students and hence narrated a story to the class and asked students to identify three new words and frame sentences from it. Ravi also presented a set of jumbled sequence of events and asked the students to arrange in the right sequence order. However, the activity was not very effective. Ravi thought of the classroom activity and identified the key challenges of the same.

Reflection:

- Ravi had narrated the story, it becomes difficult to remember the entire story in the proper sequence.
- Ravi did not explain the new words nor the meaning hence students found it difficult to remember the new words and frame sentences.
- Not all students could frame the order of the sentences of the story.

3

Models of Reflection

If you are not used to being reflective it can be hard to know where to start the process. Luckily there are many models which you can use to guide your reflection.

You will notice many common themes in these models and any others that you come across. Each model takes a slightly different approach but they all cover similar stages. The main difference is the number of steps included and how in-depth their creators have chosen to be. Different people will be drawn to different models depending on their own preferences.

ERA Cycle

The ERA cycle (Jasper, 2013) is one of the most simple models of reflection and contains only three stages:

Experience

·

Reflection

·

Action

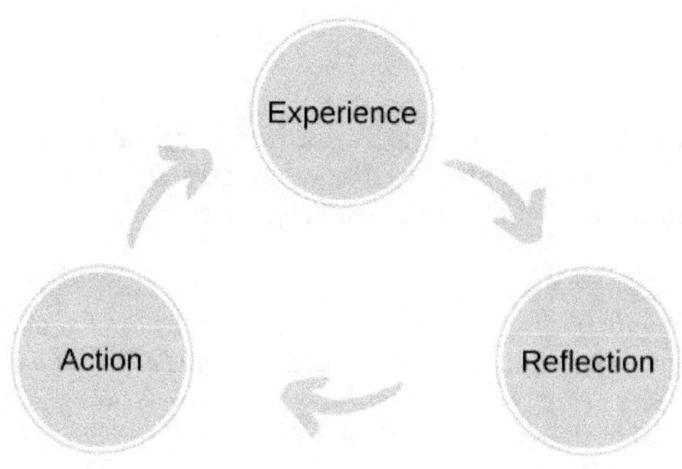

ERA Model

The cycle shows that we will start with an experience, either something we have been through before or something completely new to us. This experience can be positive or negative and may be related to our work or something else.

Once something has been experienced we will start to reflect on what happened. This will allow us to think through the experience, examine our feelings about what happened and decide on the next steps. This leads to the final element of the cycle - taking an action. What we do as a result of an experience will be different depending on the individual. This action will result in another experience and the cycle will continue.

Jasper, M. (2013). Beginning Reflective Practice. Andover: Cengage Learning.

Driscoll's What Model

Another simple model was developed by Driscoll in the mid-1990s. Driscoll based his model of the 3 What's on the key questions asked by Terry Borton in the 1970s:

- *What?*

- *So what?*

- *Now what?*

By asking ourselves these three simple questions we can begin to analyse and learn from our experiences. Firstly we should describe what the situation or experience was to set it in context. This gives us a clear idea of what we are dealing with. We should then reflect on the experience by asking 'so what?' - what did we learn as a result of the experience? The final stage asks us to think about the action we will take as a result of this reflection. Will we change a behavior, try something new or carry on as we are? It is important to remember that there may be no changes as the result of reflection and that we feel that we are doing everything as we should. This is equally valid as an outcome and you should not worry if you can't think of something to change.

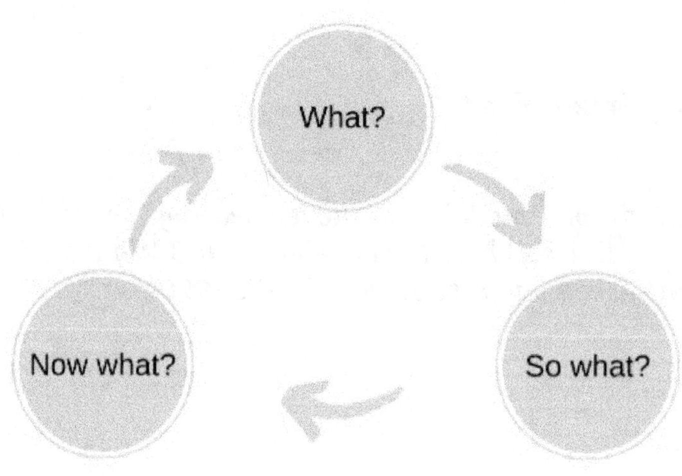

Driscoll's What Model

Borton, T. (1970) Reach, Touch and Teach. London: Hutchinson.

Driscoll, J. (ed.) (2007) Practicing Clinical Supervision: A Reflective Approach for Healthcare Professionals. Edinburgh: Elsevier.

Kolb's Experiential Learning Cycle

Kolb's model (1984) takes things a step further. Based on theories about how people learn, this model centres on the concept of developing understanding through actual experiences and contains four key stages:

- *Concrete experience*

- *Reflective observation*

- *Abstract conceptualization*

- *Active experimentation*

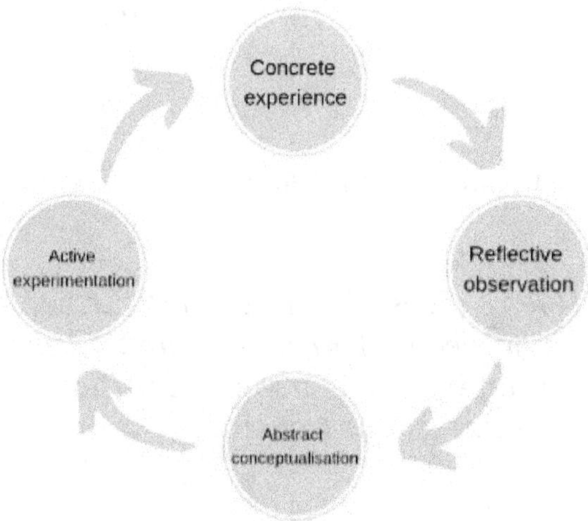

Kolb's Experiential Learning Cycle

The model argues that we start with an experience - either a repeat of something that has happened before or something completely new to us. The next stage involves us reflecting on the experience and noting anything about it which we haven't come across before. We then start to develop new ideas as a result, for example when something unexpected has happened we try to work out why this might be. The final stage involves us applying our new ideas to different situations. This demonstrates learning as a direct result of our experiences and reflections. This model is similar to one used by small children when learning basic concepts such as hot and cold. They may touch something hot, be burned and be more cautious about touching something which could potentially hurt them in the future.

Kolb, D. (1984) Experiential Learning: Experience as the Source of Learning and Development. Upper Saddle River: Prentice Hall.

Gibb's Reflective Cycle

The final model builds on the other three and adds more stages. It is one of the more complex models of reflection but it may be that you find having multiple stages of the process to guide you reassuring. Gibb's cycle contains six stages:

- *Description*

- *Feelings*

- *Evaluation*

- *Analysis*

- *Conclusion*

- *Action plan*

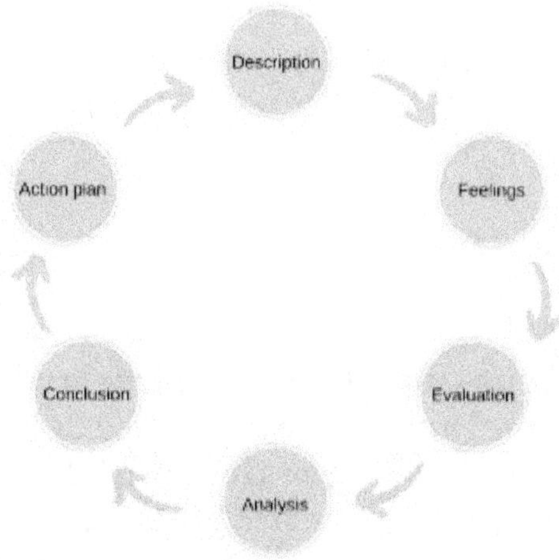

Gibb's Reflective Cycle

As with other models, Gibb's begins with an outline of the experience being reflected on. It then encourages us to focus on our feelings about the experience, both during it an after. The next step involves evaluating the experience - what was good or bad about it from our point of view? We can then use this evaluation to analyse the situation and try to make sense of it. This analysis will result in a conclusion about what other actions (if any) we could have taken to reach a different outcome. The final stage involves building an action plan of steps which we can take the next time we find ourselves in a similar situation.

Gibbs, G. (1998) Learning by Doing: A Guide to Teaching and Learning Methods. Oxford: Further Education Unit, Oxford

Polytechic.

Pros and Cons of Reflective Practice Models

A word of caution about models of reflective practice (or any other model). Although they can be a great way to start thinking about reflection, remember that all models have their downsides. A summary of the pros and cons can be found below:

Pros

- *Offer a structure to be followed*

- *Provide a useful starting point for those unsure where to begin*

- *Allow you to assess all levels of a situation*

- *You will know when the process is complete*

Cons

-

Imply that steps must be followed in a defined way

- *In the real world you may not start 'at the beginning'*

- *Models may not apply in every situation*

- *Reflective practice is a continuous process*

Conclusion

These are just some of the reflective models that are available. You may find one that works for you or you may decide that none of them really suit. These models provide a useful guide or place to start but reflection is a very personal process and everyone will work towards it in a different way. Take some time to try different approaches until you find the one that works for you. You may find that as time goes on and you develop as a reflective practitioner that you try different methods which suit your current circumstances. The important part is that it works - if it doesn't then you may need to move on and try something else.

4

Reflective teaching

Reflective teaching means looking at what you do in the classroom, thinking about why you do it, and thinking about if it works - a process of self-observation and self-evaluation. Reflective teaching is a process whereby teachers reflect on their teaching practices in order to examine the overall effectiveness of their instructive approaches. Improvement or change in teaching methods may be required, depending on the outcome of this analytical process, which is based on critical reflection.

In a simple manner, the process of reflective teaching follows a cycle which includes:

- Teaching

- Self-assessing the result of your teaching on learning by students

- *Taking into consideration other and better methods of teaching that can improve performance and the learning standards and quality*

- *Implementing these ideas into actual practice*

- *Repeating the practice again*

Reflective teachers regularly dedicate time to evaluate their teaching practice. They consider the scope of their pedagogy — from the structure of the course to the classroom community — and reflect on how their specific teaching decisions impact their students' learning. As they analyze their teaching, they consider how they might approach particular tasks or challenges in the future.

Anil was demonstrating the experiment of light in the class. However, the planned activity turned out to be unsuccessful. Anil wondered about the reasons of the failed activity.

Reflection:

- *Anil did not make the necessary arrangements in the classroom for doing the experiment*
- *Anil did not give a brief idea of the experiment.*
- *Anil might have not been effective in demonstrating.*

Classroom Experiences

Reflection questions to ask with students

• *Did this lesson help you understand other lessons better? Why?*

• *If we learn this lesson again, what can I do differently to help you learn more or better?*

• *Why was this activity successful or not successful?*

• *What did you like about this lesson?*

• *What did you dislike about this lesson?*

Reflection question about assessment and grading

• *Do my assessments reflect student learning, or just task completion and memorization skills?*

• *Do all students benefit from this learning method/activity? Who does and who doesn't? Why?*

• *Why did I choose this method/activity to cover this topic?*

• *How can I know my students are learning? Evidence?*

· *What new strategies can I try later on that might benefit a student that I'm struggling with?*

Reflection questions about classroom management

· *Do I give my student opportunities to make their own choices?*

· *Do I know my students outside of the classroom? Do I know something about their personal lives?*

· *Could pre-teaching my expectations or developing rules/ procedures help solve the problems I have in my classroom?*

· *Is the relationship that I have with my students helping/ hindering their ability to learn?*

· *Was my attitude towards my class today effective for student learning?*

Reflection questions for teachers' professional development

· *In what ways can I support my colleagues in their student's learning?*

· *In what aspects can I still improve my teaching?*

· *What's stopping me from improving in these aspects?*

· *What opportunities are there to improve myself as a teacher?*

· *Do my actions as a teacher show that I take pride in my work?*

Anita asked students to do a nature trail and write a report. However, the reports by students were not systematic nor did it follow a proper format. Anita wondered on the possible issues in reporting.

Reflection:

- *Anita did not specify the format of the report*
- *Anita did not specify the observations that was to be done during the nature trail.*
- *Anita had to be more specific in giving instructions.*

An important aspect of becoming a teacher involves beginning to think like teacher, and be aware of their practices so that the knowledge developed through the experiences of teaching and learning may be utilized to improve future practice. Reflection is one of the crucial aspects of teaching -learning process that helps the teachers to analyse their own practices and improve upon them. In fact reflecting on different aspects of teaching is fairly instinctive for most of the teachers. When confronted with a problem related to a particular session, we all try to evaluate our teaching and determine the necessary adjustments for the following session. In every teacher education program in the world, reflection is gradually becoming a fundamental requirement.

Our day-to-day lives include reflection. In scientific terms, reflection occurs when light bounces off a surface and changes direction. As a result of this reflection, we see our own reflection in the mirror. We daily reflect on a variety of issues and situations when this principle is applied to thinking. We don't have a set pattern for this, and it just happens as thoughts, feelings, and emotions about something start to come to the surface. We choose our course of action after considering various aspects of a problem or circumstance. Hence, reflection is the process of recalling, considering, and evaluating an experience in relation to a larger goal. It is a response to previous experiences and involves evaluating and making decisions based on those experiences in search of new meaning and interpretation. However, the terms "reflection" and "reflective thinking" encompass a wide range of ideas and methods. Reflective practices were practiced by Plato, Aristotle, Confucius, Solomon, and Buddha. However, this term was first coined by Dewey in the 20th century, though researchers and thinkers later deciphered the mystery surrounding it. Many current theories are based on Dewey's early work on reflection, which he published in 1916."those intellectual and affective activities in which individuals engage to explore their experiences in order to lead to new understandings and appreciations" is how Boud, Keough, and Walker (1985) define reflection. In a nutshell, reflection is the process by which a student recalls and evaluates their own experiences in order to make informed decisions. It is a way of thinking in which we consciously consider something to improve our comprehension of it. It entails noting and analyzing and synthesising the relationships between things. In other sense reflection might be considered for growing better in figuring out around oneself and for other people. The process of reflective thinking, which can be defined as the act of thinking logically or critically, results from reflection.

Reflection suggests that something is believed in or disbelieved due to evidence, proof, or reasons. It is a deliberate and active cognitive process that involves a series of interconnected ideas that take into account the knowledge and beliefs that underlie them. When dealing with practical issues, reflective thinking allows for plenty of room for skepticism, reservations, and ambiguity before arriving at potential solutions. As a result, reflective thinking can be summed up as making educated decisions based on facts and logic and then evaluating the results. It's a process that involves more than just trying to solve problems in a rational and logical way. Emotion, passion, and intuition are all part of reflection.

Teacher as Reflective Practitioner: Reflection is a process of making meaning that moves the learner from one experience to the next with a better understanding of how it relates to other experiences and ideas. It is a method of thinking that is methodical, rigorous, and disciplined and has its roots in scientific inquiry. It must take place in a group setting and with other people. It requires a mindset that values one's own and others' intellectual and personal development.

The concept of reflection has been described by Van Manen (1977) as "a progression involving three different levels-technical, practical, and critical.

The technical level is concerned with the effectiveness and efficiency of the methods used to achieve the goals, which cannot be changed or criticized. In the context of teaching and learning, it refers to the efficient application of technical knowledge and skills in the classroom.

The evaluation of educational objectives and the methods by which students achieve them are the focus of practical reflection. It makes it possible to examine openly the goals, methods, and assumptions on which they are based. As a result, this stage requires reflection on the assumptions that underlie a particular classroom practice and its effects on student learning.

The value of the educational objectives is the subject of critical reflection. It also has to do with determining who is benefiting from the achievement of these goals and how well they are being achieved. At this stage, the moral and ethical implications of decisions are questioned. Teachers at this level of reflection make connections between the broader social, political, and economic forces that influence the situations they encounter.

In 1987, Donald Schon defined reflective thinking by introducing the term "reflective practice. "Schon says that reflective practice is thinking carefully about how one has applied knowledge to practice by the teachers. Three distinct modes of reflection are included in Schon's (1987) concept of reflection. These modes include action-in reflection; action-on-reflection; and action for reflection.

Reflection-in-action

This is almost instantaneous and on-the-spot. It is generally observed that the more experienced professionals solve the problem on-the-spot. For this, they draw upon their repertoire of knowledge and skills to understand the situation. In other words, rather than randomly trying any other approach, the professionals use their accumulated experience and knowledge to address the problem instantly.

Reflection-on-action

This occurs after the action has taken place in the classroom. It is a deliberate and conscious process, involving a greater critical analysis of the action and looking back at the problem or event.

Reflection-for-action

This is said to be a desired proactive outcome for both "reflection-in-action" and "reflection- on-action". It is the process of analysing events and behaviour, with the sole purpose of making changes in the future. The purpose of reflection, more so of, reflective practice, is not merely to think about past events, experiences, or behaviour, but also to guide a positive future action. Teachers can practice "reflection- for-action" to prepare for the future, by assessing the information gathered from what actually happened in the class and what they reflected upon after the class. This would also allow them to identify any dissonance, between their beliefs and actual practices. Teachers who practise "reflection-for-action" are able to move forward from focusing on non-desirable events and experiences of the present, and concentrate on how to change the situation into what they want it to be. This gives them an action plan for the future.

Reflection-within

This is inquiring about personal purposes, intentions and feelings. Teachers might question what is working well, what's keeping them from taking action, what's keeping their perspective limited, or why they reacted in a particular way. This is very similar to self-reflection.

Reflection: an ongoing Personal Process

Reflection is a continuous process. You need to reflect upon your teaching practice, on a continuing basis, throughout your career, since there is always scope for improvement in teaching practice. Besides, reflection is a process which is personal.

> Prerna planned for a role play, she assigned role and gave the students narration for the role play. The students performed the role play however there was no co-ordination in the entire act. Prerena was disappointed and thought of the possible reasons.
>
> ## Reflection:
>
> - Prerna had planned for the role play, however before the final act, she could have done a rehearsal and looked into the presentation of the role play.
> - Prerna during the rehearsal could have identified the roles assigned to the students were duly suitable.

Classroom Experiences

Major Components of Reflection

The concept of reflection, as discussed above, highlights its major elements as follows:

• conditions, situations, or circumstances prompting engagement in the reflective process;

• processes, types, concepts, or opinions on how this is undertaken;

• content, what exactly needs to be analysed, examined, discussed, challenged in the reflective process, and with what perspectives or ideologies; and

• product, improved understanding of professional practice and/or action as a result of reflective thinking.

Reflective teaching

This means looking at what you do in the classroom, thinking about why you do it, and thinking about it if works as a process of self-observation and self- evaluation. Reflective teaching is a cyclical process; and once you start to implement changes, the reflective and evaluative cycle begins.

Traits of a Reflective Teacher

Understanding reflective practice as a concept is crucial. In order to be clear about what it means and in order to understand reflective teaching, it is necessary to emphasise five key features as traits of a reflective teacher, who:

- *examines, frames, and attempts to solve the problems of classroom practice;*

- *is aware of and questions the assumptions and values entailing teaching;*

- *is attentive to the institutional and cultural contexts in which to perform;*

- *takes part in curriculum development and is involved in the efforts to bring change; and*

- *takes responsibility for one's own professional development*

Self Assessment :

Self-Assessment: Are You a Reflective Teacher? Think about yourself regarding the following elements of reflective teaching. Respond to each statement by writing always, often, sometimes, rarely, or never.

1. I examine my own reactions to children and their actions to understand where they come from. ___________________

2. I pause after an activity or at the end of the day to examine whether my practice had a positive impact on children's learning and development. ___________________

3. I ask co-workers and children's families for their insights. ___________________

4. I eagerly share stories about children's learning with families and coworkers. ___________________

5. I have captured my practice on video, viewed it and analyzed my practice to notice strengths and plan for improvement. ___________________

6. I am curious about children's play and watch it closely. ___________________

7. I document details of children's conversations and activities and take time to study the notes and photos to puzzle out what's significant about them. ___________________

8. *I read professional literature to learn more.* ___________________

9. *I show children photos and stories of themselves to hear their views.* ___________________

10. *I use my observations and reflections to change the environment and materials to encourage new play and learning possibilities.* ___________________

Characteristics of Reflective Teaching

The characteristics of reflective teaching are as follows:

1. The ability to reflect upon one's teaching practice and identify the strengths and weaknesses from it.

2. Focusing on self-improvement for better teaching practices as well as for professional growth.

3. It is based on the teacher's self-observation and self-evaluation of their teaching methods.

4. Open-mindedness towards one's teaching practices and willingness to improve for the best.

Importance of Reflective Teaching

The importance of reflective teaching are as mentioned below:

1. Reflective teaching helps the teachers in understanding their performance and improving it for the better future of the students.

2. Reflective teaching leads to innovative methods and techniques of teaching by the educator. It allows teachers to find innovative ways to make the class activities interesting and fun for the students. This way students will receive satisfying class lessons.

3. Reflective teaching also helps in the improvement of the teacher's problem-solving skills. They will be able to come up with new techniques and strategies to make the learning process easy and simple for the students to understand.

4. Reflective teaching allows the teacher to be responsible towards his/her duty and take the student's future seriously.

Approaches of Reflective Teaching

The approaches of reflective teaching are the following:

- *Self-reflection and self-assessment.*

- *Request for student and peer feedback*

- *Recording class lessons of self for observation.*

- *Use innovative teaching methods and techniques.*

- *Come up with new teaching techniques and strategies.*

- *Build a good relationship with the students.*

Reflective teaching is an important concept. It can help a teacher largely in the way he/she functions in the classroom. Reflective teaching allows us to know what works best for the interest of the students. This will lead to both effective teaching and the learning process.

Approaches to Reflective Thinking:

In the context of teachers' reflective thinking, the literature on reflective thinking describes three general approaches: the cognitive, critical, and narrative approach.

Cognitive approach *is relevant to teachers' decision-making and information processing; whereas ethical and moral reasoning are the foundations of the critical approach. Through problem framing, case studies, naturalistic inquiry, and other methods, the narrative approach refers to teachers telling their own stories (narratives). The cognitive approach places an emphasis on the organization of the knowledge base into networks of related facts, ideas, generalizations, and experiences.*

Critical Pedagogy Approach *sees knowledge as something that is made in a social setting. The critical approach examines teachers' experiences, values, and goals in terms of their socio-political implications, whereas the cognitive approach emphasizes how teachers make decisions. Critical pedagogy is frequently compared to the critical approach. For instance, "learning to listen to others" may be more important to some children than encouraging them to speak up in class for others. Therefore, teachers must consider the long-term impact of teaching methods on students' values and perceptions and visualize teaching as an inquiry process.*

Narrative Approach *"the voices of teachers themselves, the questions teachers ask, the way teachers use writing and intentional talk in their work life and interpretative frames teachers use to understand and improve their own classroom practices are what is missing from the knowledge base of teaching." Teachers' own descriptions of the personal circumstances under which they make decisions are emphasized in this approach. As they describe, analyze, and draw conclusions from classroom activities, teachers develop their own pedagogical principles.*

Reflective teaching can be enhanced through:

1) Aid the students in identifying his or her learning needs.

2) Provide students with multiple points of view on the issue at hand;

3) Make it easier for students to find worthwhile experiences;

4) Facilitate students in-depth reflection on these experiences.

Teacher narratives, keeping reflective journals, thinking aloud, discussions, collaborative group projects, action research, role playing, brainstorming, buzz groups, and other methods can all help teachers foster reflective thinking. Questioning is perhaps one of the oldest of these methods, allowing students and teachers to meaningfully reflect on various aspects of the topic at hand that would otherwise be overlooked. It also helps students identify problems, clarify values, and develop a deep understanding of the issue, among other things.

Raj gave a group activity on renewable and non-renewable resources; the group activity was not successful. Raj pondered on the possible causes for the same.

Reflection:

- *Raj could have guided the students in-depth before the group activity.*
- *Raj could have assigned roles within the group.*
- *Raj could have selected and prepared identical groups.*
- *Raj could have assigned specific topics for each groups.*

Classroom Experiences

5

Reflective classroom practices

—♡—

Attitudes

Dewey was the first to describe the 3 attitudes that form the basis of reflective practice, namely:

- *Open-mindedness - a willingness to consider new evidence as it occurs and to admit the possibility of error. It involves being open to other points of view, appreciating that there are many ways of looking at a particular situation or event, and staying open to changing one's own viewpoint. Part of open-mindedness is being able to let go of needing to be right or wanting to win.*

- *Responsibility - the careful consideration of the consequences of one's actions, especially as they affect students. It is the willingness to acknowledge that whatever one chooses to do (for example decisions about curriculum, instruction, assessment, organisation, management) will impact on the lives of students in both foreseen and unforeseen ways.*

Wholeheartedness - a commitment to seek every opportunity to learn and a belief that one can always learn something new.

Nitin presented a PPT on Demand and Determinants of Demand to students of Class IX. The PPT was full of text matter and was conceptual. Nitin read the matter on the PPT. Later asked few questions. Students couldn't answer the questions. Nitin reflected on the classroom activity.

Reflection:

- *Nitin had loaded the PPT with content which was difficult for students to grasp the matter.*
- *Nitin could have mentioned only the bullet point or key concepts and also explained the content with adequate examples.*
- *Nitin could have planned the recap questions as per the content and it could be linked to the learning outcomes.*

Classroom Experiences

Attributes

Larivee further identified the attributes of practitioners who have these attitudes (open-minded, responsible and wholehearted) saying these practitioners:

- *reflect on and learn from experience*

- *engage in ongoing inquiry*

- *solicit feedback*

- *remain open to alternative perspectives*

- *assume responsibility for their own learning*

- *take action to align with new knowledge and understandings*

- *observe themselves in the process of thinking*

- *are committed to continuous improvement in practice*

- *strive to align behaviour with values and beliefs*

-

seek to discover what is true.

.

Lenses for reflection

Additionally, within each mode of reflection, it's useful to reflect through various lenses. Brookfield suggests using the following 4 lenses for reflection.

Lenses for Reflection

The autobiographical lens (self)

The autobiographical lens, or self-reflection, is the foundation of critical reflection. It requires teachers to stand back from an experience and view it more objectively. This lens allows teachers to become aware of aspects of their pedagogy that are effective or that may need adjustment or strengthening.

The student lens

*This lens allows teachers to view their practice from students'
perspectives and is often a consistently surprising element
for teachers. Both self-reflection and engaging with student
feedback may reveal aspects of teaching practice that need
adjustment.*

The colleague lens

*While good teachers will engage with the first two lenses,
excellent teachers may also look to peers for mentoring,
advice and feedback. Engaging with colleagues and hearing
their perspectives allows teachers to check, reframe, and
broaden theories of practice, and to consider new ideas and
approaches. It also makes teachers aware that many of the
challenges in teaching are common, which can be profoundly
reassuring.*

The theoretical lens (literature and research)

*The fourth lens found in theoretical literature fosters
critically reflective teaching. An engagement with both
colleagues and scholarly literature supports teachers and also*

clarifies the contexts in which they teach. The theoretical literature extends understanding and appreciation of learning and teaching practices, and helps teachers to see the links between their personal development path and the broader educational context.

Reflective Teaching Examples

Self-Assessment

Reflection Journals: Instructors might consider capturing a few details of their teaching in a journal to create an ongoing narrative of their teaching across terms and years. Scheduling a dedicated time during the 5 or so minutes after class to write their entries will ensure continual engagement, rather than hoping to find a moment throughout the day. The instructor writes general thoughts about the day's lesson and might reflect on the following questions: What went well today? What could I have done differently? How will I modify my instruction in the future?

Teaching Inventories: A number of inventories, like the Teaching Practices Inventory have been developed to help instructors assess and think more broadly about their teaching approaches. Inventories are typically designed to assess the extent to which particular pedagogies are employed (e.g. student- versus teacher-centered practices).

Video-Recorded Teaching Practices: Teachers can video record their lessons while conducting a classroom observation, or instructors can video record themselves while teaching and use a classroom observation protocol to self-assess their own practices.

Teaching Portfolio: A more time-intensive practice, the teaching portfolio invites instructors to integrate the various components of their teaching into a cohesive whole, typically starting with a teaching philosophy or statement, moving through sample syllabi and assignments, and ending with evaluations from colleagues and students. Though less focused on classroom practices, a portfolio is an opportunity to reflect on teaching overall.

Examples of External Assessment

Student Evaluations (Midterm and End-of-Term): In many courses, instructors obtain feedback from students in the form of mid-semester feedback and/or end-of-term student evaluations. They can seek out other ways to assess their practices to accompany student evaluation data before taking steps to modify instruction.

Peer Review of Teaching: Instructors can ask a trusted colleague to observe their classroom and give them feedback on their teaching. Colleagues can agree on an observation protocol or a list of effective teaching principles to focus on from a teaching practices inventory.

Classroom Observations: Observations are meant to be non-evaluative and promote reflection. They begin with a discussion in which the instructor describes course goals and format as well as any issues or teaching practices that are of primary concern. This initial discussion provides useful context for the observation and the post-observation conversation.

Presentations: A way for students to share their service-learning experience with peers is to make a class presentation through a video, slide show, bulletin board, panel discussion, or a persuasive speech. This is an opportunity for students to display their work in a public format. A similar presentation can be offered to the community agency as a final recognition of the students' involvement.

Directed Readings: Directed readings are a way to prompt students to consider their service experience within a broader context of social responsibility and civic literacy. Since textbooks rarely challenge students to consider how knowledge within a discipline can be applied to current social needs, additional readings must be added if this is a learning objective of the course. Directed readings can become the basis for class discussion or a directed writing.

Ethical Case Studies: Ethical case studies give students the opportunity to analyze a situation and gain practice in ethical decision making as they choose a course of action. This reflection strategy can foster the exploration and clarification of values. Students write a case study of an ethical dilemma they have confronted at the service site, including a description of the context, the individuals involved, and the controversy or event that created an ethical dilemma.

Student Portfolios: This type of documentation has become a vital way for students to keep records and learn organizational skills. Encourage them to take photographs of themselves doing their project, short explanations (like business reports), time logs, evaluations by supervisors or any other appropriate "proof" which could be used in an interview. Require them to make this professional. Keep reminding them that submitting it at the end of the term is only one reason for doing this. "The real reason is to have documentation to present at future interviews. This could be a major factor in distinguishing them from other candidates." Student portfolios could contain any of the following: service-learning contract, weekly log, personal journal, impact statement, directed writings, photo essay.

Ann played a video of a conversation between two American experts on Thinking skills. The video was played to a group of students who were first generation learners. Ann realised that the students were not paying attention to the video conversation. Ann reflected on the planned classroom activity.

Reflection:

- *Ann was playing the video to the first generation learners and the conversation was in English which was difficult to understand and decipher.*
- *The communication / presentation of the content would have been fluent and at a specific speed, this would have been difficult for the first generation learners.*
- *The students lost interest in the video presentation as it was not as per the level of their understanding.*

Classroom Experiences

6

Classroom Experiences

Ganesh dictated notes in the class of Std III. Ganesh took the books for correction and found the matter incomplete and lot of spelling mistakes. Ganesh reflected on the task done by him.

Reflection:

- *Ganesh would have dictated the content in a pace that would have been difficult for young students to write.*
- *Generally the students of Std III will need guided practice, hence writing it from the blackboard would have been easier.*
- *The students of Std III may not be thorough with the spellings hence it would cause errors.*

Classroom Experiences

Rita encouraged brainstorming session in the class. Only few students responded to it. Rita wondered the reason for low response from students.

Reflection:

- Rita had to choose an appropriate topic for brainstorming,
- Rita had to choose an age and understanding appropriate topic.
- Rita had to create interest in the activity and encourage all students to participate by calling their names, roll numbers or make groups, concept maps etc.

Classroom Experiences

Std IX - A of a school has 68 students. The class is very crowded, the students are quite grown up and their huge bags makes the mobility in class restricted to a large extent. Vivek has been noticing disciplinary issues in the class and has been reflecting on the reasons for indiscipline.

Reflection:

- *Vivek needs to take efforts in classroom seating arrangement.*
- *Vivek needs to devise activities that would encourage more of desk jobs.*
- *Vivek need to focus on rotation of seating arrangements.*
- *Vivek need to focus on plan movement in the class so that the teachers can even focus on all the corners of the class.*

Classroom Experiences

Farah, computer teacher has given surfing time for students of class VI, she has noticed most of the students resort to playing games during that time. She is thinking of ways to change the habits of the students.

Reflection:

- *Farah needs to plan for games and activities that will encourage in enhancing academic skills among students.*
- *Farah needs to plan for pre-decided tasks that has to be done by students during their computer class.*
- *Farah needs to constantly monitor the students activities through regular checks.*
- *Farah needs to block the websites giving access to the games and other forbidden sites.*

Classroom Experiences

Radha encourages students to develop reading skills. Everyday the last 10 minutes of her lecture she dedicates in group reading. However, the reading of all her students are not well developed. Radha thinks of the reasons.

Reflection:

- *Radha focuses on group reading, hence she is not aware if all the children are doing the reading task appropriately.*
- *Radha's group reading task does not focus on pronunciation as the same is not addressed well.*
- *Radha's group reading does not cater to all learners.*

Classroom Experiences

Kumar covertly bangs on the bottom of his desk, making distracting noises while you are teaching. When you ask him to stop, he looks innocent and claims he is not doing anything. And yet when you go back to teaching, he continues the noise again.

Reflection:

- *As a teacher in the class, the behaviour of Kumar is distracting your teaching-learning process, hence you will find out the reason for the same.*
- *You will find out if Kumar does the same action in other lectures.*
- *You will talk to Kumar and find out the reasons for the same.*
- *You may change Kumar's seating position.*
- *You may even talk to few other students in the class about Kumar's behaviour.*

Classroom Experiences

Ms. Geeta believes students need to be empowered by making choices and setting goals. She has had very good experiences with most of the students. However, there are a few that are really hard to reach. She has days where they set goals and achieve them and days when they do nothing, just a little bit, or just enough to get by. Her usual procedure is to have students decide on a task, how to do it, and supporting them while they work (plan, do, review or state of the classroom). When they are done she usually gives them feedback, feed forward, and praise for their accomplishments.

Reflection:

- *Ms. Geeta has to plan her learning outcomes as per the students ability and understanding.*
- *Ms. Geeta needs to be flexible in her approach and can believe that there are two sides of the coin.*
- *Ms. Geeta needs to be patient and let the learning happen in a learner centric manner.*

Deepak believes students must be active if they are to learn, generalize, and be able to solve real life problems. He also believes students learn by communicating their ideas and that what they need to learn is not always in a textbook. At the beginning of the year things seemed to go pretty good. Lately the productivity of the students seems to have decreased. Students take longer to decide what they are going to do, who is going to do what, and argue about it. When they see that the allotted time is about to expire, they make hasty decisions and complete the task quickly, which reduces the quality of work.

Reflection:

- *Deepak needs to plan of goal setting activities for student to be updated and keeping them abreast with the life situations.*
- *Deepak can arrange for counselling sessions.*
- *Deepak can adopt mew methods of teaching that will enhance collaborative learning, active learning.*
- *Deepak needs to keep frequent formative assessment for students.*

Classroom Experiences

Priya begins each class by asking students what they know about a topic, reviewing past learnings, explaining what students are to do, making an assignment, asking students what questions they have, and letting the students work. The same students volunteer ideas while others are not very attentive and do not volunteer answers. When she has completed her instruction and students are working on an assignment she roams the room and helps students with individual problems. As she helps she is constantly checking to see if students are on task and if not dealing with them before helping others. She also is able to check on students who may have trouble, based on her understanding of the student's needs and assessment data. Lately there seems to be more students who seek help, some who finish very quickly, and a general decrease in the quality of about half of the students' work.

The early finishers talk, pass notes, walk around the class and visit. Occasionally a student will engage in a silly behavior behind her back and make the rest of the class giggle.

Reflection:

- *Priya need to plan her lesson well and involve students in group activities and distribute the task based on the level of the child and the learning spaces.*
- *Priya can be more specific in classroom acceptable behaviour and should insist in adhering the same.*
- *Priya need to focus on learning outcomes after each class and measure the same through formative class assessment.*

Classroom Experiences

Govid has been trying to get through several of the objectives which are part of the school district's curriculum. He has repeatedly told students that the material will be on the test and has wondered if they really understand the seriousness of what he has been trying to tell them for three days. When he gave the test his thoughts were confirmed. When he talked to them as a group, they claimed they knew it and they have been paying attention in class. They claimed that the test was unfair because it was confusing and they did not understand for sure what he wanted.

Reflection:

- *Govind needs to do regular formative assessment that will help him to gauge the achievement of learning outcomes by students.*
- *Govind can also give students Practice Test papers and discuss the sample questions with expected answers.*
- *Govind can give constructive feedback to students for improvement in grades.*

Classroom Experiences

You've assigned on-line discussion groups. You are reviewing student postings and discover inappropriate language and sexual references to persons being discussed.

Reflection:

- *The teacher needs to have a session on online etiquettes.*
- *The teacher needs to take strict action against inappropriate language demeaning others self respect.*
- *The teacher needs to be firm in limiting the expected responses on topics.*

Classroom Experiences

References

https://poorvucenter.yale.edu/
ReflectiveTeaching#:~:text=Reflective%20teaching

https://reflectiveteachingjournal.com/what-is-reflective-teaching/

https://www.teachingenglish.org.uk/article/reflective-teaching-exploring-our-

own-classroom-practice

https://www.teachmint.com/glossary/r/reflective-teaching/

https://www.richmondshare.com.br/what-is-reflective-teaching-and-why-is-it-important/

https://apiar.org.au/wp-content/uploads/2017/02/13

https://reflectiveteachingjournal.com/benefits-of-reflective-teaching/

https://egyankosh.ac.in/handle/123456789/7270

https://egyankosh.ac.in/handle/123456789/46594

https://ncert.nic.in/dte/pdf/Reflective_Teaching-13221.pdf

https://www.studocu.com/in/document/mahatma-gandhi-university/

Disclaimer:

The information provided in this book is for informational purposes only and is not intended to be a source of advice or credit analysis with respect to the material presented. The author does not make any guarantee or other promise as to any results that may be obtained from using the content of this book. The author assume no responsibility for errors, inaccuracies, omissions, or any other inconsistencies herein and hereby disclaim any liability to any party for any loss, damage, or disruption caused by errors or omissions, whether such errors or omissions result from negligence, accident, or any other cause.